King of the Hill

by

Marc Bernard Lavallee

RoseDog Books
PITTSBURGH, PENNSYLVANIA 15238

RoseDog Books
585 Alpha Drive, Suite 103
Pittsburgh, PA 15238
Visit our website at *www.rosedogbookstore.com*

ISBN: 978-1-4809-6373-3
eISBN: 978-1-4809-6395-5

To Susy

1

Intro, Into the Purpose of Life

There is a child's game popular with some, and possibly with many, which is a great model of the world in which we live. The game is called King of the Hill.

In the game, which models life, the players scramble to be "on the top;" the players play for the top of a hill. It involves obtaining a rush from a false idea of power, from being "on the top." In reality those who play the game create chaos, chaos that is founded on much conflict and fighting. The game is an especially accurate model of real life because of the conflict created and fighting that goes on in life in striving to be "on the top". It's a struggle to do the right thing, to seek God in all a person does, not just in the company of "kings" or "successful" people, those in competition to dominate any aspect of their lives, which marks the difference between those who do and do not play.

The people of the adult version of King of the Hill pursue an imaginary "hill," – a hill that turns out to be quite transient. It's sad when people pursue the transient, or, they support others in their attempt to reach it, because transient things have little value in comparison to the spiritual and the eternal. By seeking joy as opposed to say seeking happiness, by being just and charitable, by doing their part in the salvation plan, a person can reach the only "Hill" that matters, Heaven.

God does not wish His children to dominate each other, or to fight, or even to compete; He just wants His children to live for Him and others, where everybody has an identity that is empowering to those around. Truly why would anyone play a game that creates chaos and involves fighting, which is done in real life by adults, when God wills us to live for others, especially if such behavior only causes pain and is extremely not necessary? (In fact it's do to the fact that because the behavior of King of the Hill is acted out by adults all over the world that the game exists). The greatest temptation is to retreat or attempt to retreat from the world of King of the Hill altogether. The hard thing to do, which happens to be the right thing to do, is to do what you can to change the world "from within it."

In the Bible almost all of Jesus' miracles appear to be either to display the power of God or to show the immense compassion He and His Father had for humanity. God designed the human heart for compassion, a God-given skill that can be developed all throughout life. Being compassionate involves work, but the kind of work that has real benefits. Arguably the most important benefit is joy. An inherent additional problem exists with trying to reach the transient "Hill" "real life" players pursue because the actions of those trying to reach it lack compassion. People need to follow Christ's example of compassion as often as necessary, to do their part in the salvation plan. The most compassionate thing we, God's children, can do, after being moral with our person, is to peacefully protest "real life" players of King of the Hill, to ensure justice and peace. Being just and charitable does this.

In one story from the bible there is a rich man who approaches Jesus and inquires as to what else he can do to enter the Kingdom of Heaven other than being moral in personal morality, the greatest form of morality. After answering Jesus that he does keep the commandments Jesus then asks the rich man to sell all that he has, give it to the poor, and follow him. The point of the story is that morals relating to one's private life, like the Ten Commandments, are very important. However, if not as important is how one is being compassionate, if one's actions are in an attempt to establish justice and peace; there are many people who are very moral in their personal lives but when it comes to peace and justice are very corrupt, like the rich man in the Bible, like when he couldn't give of himself completely (charity).

The King of the Hill world is one where humans are judged bad or good people depending upon whether they are successful or not. In the world of winners and losers, or of the successful and the unsuccessful, if a person is considered bad or good, from being characterized as a winner and loser, or from being considered as successful or unsuccessful, there are only losers and the unsuccessful. For those who wish to create a different world, where everyone is considered valuable, where one's goal is to empower each and any possible person one can there is peace. The worst byproducts of the King of the Hill world are events like each and every war, the terrorists' actions of 9/11/01, abortion, violent protests against abortion, all the school shootings in the

US, and the bombing at the Boston Marathon on April 15th, 2013. One must work with all moral might to not be in some way responsible for such senseless acts. Any kind of violent protest, or effort to change with violence, is an example of the exact thing you should be spending your life trying to change. It's the person who is moral in their private life, and in relation to the peaceful protest of the adult version of King of the Hill, who can truly be described as a loving individual who completely follows Christ. Through good morals and by peacefully protesting the King of the Hill would, with the Grace of God, a person can reach the only hill that matters, Heaven.

2

Intro to Golden Rule Theme

Compassion is indeed an order from God, a moral standard. To be compassionate in the world of the King of the Hill is to follow a moral standard from God. The Catholic Church calls this moral standard the Golden Rule.

The Golden Rule calls a person to love God and neighbor. Jesus gives us the Golden Rule through His disciples and the Bible. By following sound Christian morals defined by the Golden Rule, both personally and socially, a person is protesting the adult version of King of the Hill.

Protesting the adult version of King of the Hill is, indeed, the second best moral act that a person can do in life, after good personal morality, in doing the most a person can do to be with Christ in Heaven. By following the Golden Rule a person is doing the most he or she can do to work for his or her salvation. Following the Golden Rule is the quest to reduce personal glorification to exude the love of the Christ and obtain His Glorification.

If a person lives the Golden Rule that person can be described as a person who truly lives. To truly live is to have an identity that defines differently the person from the players of the adult version of King of the Hill, which very often means being among the minority.

The person who follows the Golden Rule, for example, is a person who works to lead the world in the right direction from the direction in which it is, and has always been, in. These people are able to work for peace and justice in the world because they know the utmost importance of the Golden Rule in connection to their personal relationship with God. In fact, things like joy and inner peace are possible because a person has a personal relationship with God. Moreover having a strong relationship with God is more important than bringing peace to the world. However the point made here is that people can protest the adult version of King of the Hill, and establish a strong personal relationship with Him. Working for just wages and being charitable is a great part of the this work.

Indeed people who are moral and loving, so as to obtain favor with God, which is to build up the strength of their relationship with Him, are not overly despaired by the fact that achieving Heaven on earth is not possible. The joy these people experience from their personal relationships with God and the snippets of peace through justice they encounter, when they share the company of others of the same faith in prayer and in celebration, are very inspirational toward working for justice and peace. It's the beauty of being with others of the same Christian faith, in person and/or in Spirit that is the driving force behind the people who follow the Golden Rule. The most important thing to remember here is that no one is excluded from being eligible to be a neighbor – there are no "others."

Neighbors are not just others of the same race, education level, profession, company, military, country, and or culture. A neighbor is all of the people of each of these groups and anyone who doesn't neatly fall into any of them. And one's neighbor is not just a person or persons a person likes, or with whom one shares the same beliefs. If a person has any at all a neighbor is even all of one's enemies, as hard as that might be to except.

All are called to live the Golden Rule. In fact, even though being Christian isn't important to a greater percentage of people than people are willing to accept, a person can not say that he or she is a Christian if he or she does not live the Golden Rule. Furthermore, one can not live the Golden Rule halfheartedly. A person either loves God and neighbor or they don't. It's to live the Golden Rule halfheartedly is not to live it at all.

3

Country/Family, Christianity and King of the Hill

People seem to be obsessed with being patriotic despite the moral consequences of so doing. Obviously, a threat to a person's moral integrity doesn't arise when someone thinks of their country as an extension of their family. A problem arises when a person is unable to see all threats to their moral integrity because of their patriotism, when they can't look on their nationality objectively, not admitting their nation's imperfections, and responsibility, for example, for injustice in the world. It's when people from all socioeconomic statuses work side by side to secure a nation's wealth and/or corrupt status, in particular, when the effort is not founded on Christian conduct, that there is a problem; the problem is that the majority of each country gives in to "blind" patriotism.

People should honor those who have shown, and continue to show, love for their country by being as Christ-like as they can be; no one should settle for the state of affairs in one's country, and/or the world, as the best that can be when world culture and politics is as non-Christian as they are.

A family must try and be strong for the world and not expect that the world will be strong for it. In the end a person's first responsibility is to their Christian family, not as a citizen of any particular country.

Indeed, it's not just the rich and powerful who are responsible for injustice and conflict within a country and/or in the world. It's people of every socioeconomic group that fail to evaluate each and every person as a neighbor, worthy of justice and charity, who is responsible for conflict and war. Furthermore, the government, the economy, and the military, of each and every country, are such because the masses authorize and condone their make-up; the masses allow the government, the economy, and the military to have the power they have, and, oftentimes, tragically, to protect a philosophy and mentality, and a behavior that doesn't protect them.

The masses are not governed but are co-conspirators to conflict and war when each and every person from a country doesn't put into practice loving one's neighbor. For to be Christian is to love all mankind, even one's enemies. People are especially co-conspirators when they join the military and fight for the governments that don't defend the poor of the world. Being "enabling" co-conspirators, through behaving according to the principals of anti-Christian popular cultures in the world, is the biggest building block of the King of the Hill world, in which we live.

Indeed, many people who join the military are protecting a system that doesn't focus on the Golden rule which is to defend the poor and those with no power, wealth, and/or influence, all God-centered monetarily poor people in the world who, because of greed and other sins against the family, are struggling to survive.

One by-law which stems from the Golden Rule should be if harm doesn't come your way don't seek it out. Military members shouldn't support a system that doesn't allow all to benefit, all the members of your country, and the world, even those who don't benefit from wealth and status. These soldiers need to realize that most wars could be prevented if only everybody within a country was just and charitable and were not concentrating mostly on wealth, power, and/or status. Any such soldier needs to retreat and learn the art of defense, they must go all the way back to the most important entity, their soul and make sure it's pure. And countries can't worry about our nation being strong.

Most governments, in theory, are supposed to work for the people, at least those of their particular country. The discarded truth is that many times they don't. Take for example when the U.S. government bails out large corporations from eventual failure or when governments from poor countries don't stress the importance of being economically ready to have children, within the context of the nuclear family, before having children. Government bailouts, or corporate welfare, most of the time, don't protect the lowest of the company, the unskilled. And inappropriate childbearing is irresponsible and damaging, both to children and the economy. With corporate welfare the low level workers, the unskilled of the company, aren't protected, and when governments don't advocate for the nuclear family and responsible childbearing more low level workers are created. Furthermore the unskilled workers know if they do "raise a stink" the effort will almost always be futile and/or they will never be able to find jobs with trying to "seek" justice. All the while the wealth of the rich in trades and companies, like those who make up the boards of executives of companies, is protected.

No government of any country should force people to follow any particular religion. However, every person within a government and country should be moral and loving in a Christ-like fashion. It doesn't matter if the people running a country are liberal or conservative, neither if from a Communist or Democratic country (Communistic countries can't take God out of the picture and the people of capitalistic nations can't fall into mind set that wealth and power signifies they, or their nation, is of God's elect). The problem is just that, people worldwide aren't ashamed of being overtly anti-Christian.

The truth is that there has never been a government, and/or army for that matter, that has mostly worked and/or fought for God-centered people. True Christians are waiting for the day when governments and armies work for God-centered people and not the greedy and/or corrupt, particularly the monetarily poor but rich in the Holy Spirit, worldwide (The paradox, however, is that true Christians don't want anyone to fight for them.) Indeed people need to understand that defense, as defined by the Universal Church, arguably, never has been the reason why wars have been fought. For example, as a general rule, rich members of companies must advocate for the poor members of companies, without fear of losing jobs and/or being ostracized, even if the poor members are foreigners, even foreigners working in factories in foreign countries; people need to reconsider what being Catholic(for all people in the world) really means.

Simply put, if a person calls themselves Christian they must work for their neighbor in all manner possible, particularly by shedding all things worldly, one's wealth, one's popularity, and, if God has it as a plan for you, even your life. A person can't worry about being brandished as something very unduly named, like what happens in the US when someone speaks of justice; Immediately that person is called a communist, which is branded automatically by lazzie-faire capitalists who seek to abuse (or continue to abuse) workers. Anything intelligible and loving will point you toward the inaccuracy of such claims by those who use and abuse. And by doing so you will truly help your country/family find peace.

4

Justice and Charity, and the Purpose of Material Possessions

Indeed it's tough to change the problems that derive from the King of the Hill mentality because people from all socioeconomic groups engage in them, and countries of all wealth's, the rich, a majority of the poor, and even many people from the middle class, both people from the right, the middle, and the left. It's hard to say, for example, that the rich are unjust and greedy if the poor and middle classes support and/or permit them to be unjust and greedy, or when both Republicans and Democrats are rich.

The problem with injustice in the world becomes even more difficult to correct when people are willing to kill for their nation that has many faults, countries that protect and permit the greedy to be greedy, or Communist nations who use a majority of others to achieve their domination goals. Additionally, it's sad when killing, secures for a lot people the closest thing to worldly power that life on earth can provide, like that is all they have to offer the world.

People who make up governments forget what's really important, which is protecting the poor not using them. Governments have even gone to the extreme of conscripting people to protect their wealth or immoral worldly status, or paying people to be outright assassins. By being just, like Christ wants of us is the fastest way to be with Him and the Heavenly Father, and to know everlasting joy. It's only from working to obtain a "position" in Heaven can a person know true greatness, joy, and peace.

It is very true when people say that when you die you can't take wealth and popularity with you. Why people refuse to accept that truth is both sad and disappointing at the same time. Many such persons don't have faith, and seek an identity in hoarding wealth and/or status, and don't see the value in Christian justice, charity, and love. It is especially hard to embrace Christian justice, charity, and love when pursuing them means being counter-cultural, and apart from most people, to point where your friendships, career, and even your health could be at risk.

It's paradoxical that rich and powerful have so much yet still feel so poor and/or empty. And how some poor people, those who work for the Kingdom of Heaven, feel as though they have everything. It's almost as if, if you're poor/and powerless you have the option of being rich and/or influential, but if you're rich and/or powerful, you don't have the option of truly being rich and/or influential. Additionally, the desire and motivation to be rich and/or powerful (successful) in and for themselves is, also, dangerous.

The reality of the relationship between material possessions and happiness is a paradox that exists because, again, material possessions are only there to aid a person in becoming a child of God and not are there to be acquired excessively and hoarded, especially when considering that God-centered people worldwide are without the bare necessities in life to live well; it's only by becoming a child of God a person can acquire inner peace.

Jesus through the Bible defines charity, when he used a parable of a rich man and poor woman donating at the Temple. The simple truth people with excess and power don't understand, or except, is that they can use their wealth and/or positions of authority to do God's will or not, justly or charitably.

A person with a million dollars giving one thousand dollars in charity is not nearly as charitable as a person with ten thousand dollars giving one thousand dollars in charity; charity is when a person gives a great percent of themselves, their wealth, time, and talent. And if a person doesn't work for the transformation of their enemies into neighbors worthy of charity that person doesn't understand what Jesus is all about. Many people who hoard excess wealth and/or work to control others don't understand that God, who demands of us to be just and charitable, is the source of all wealth and power.

Little do rich hoarders and people who value anti-Christian worldliness know, the best way to know joy is to give up all desire for worldly riches and anti-Christian repute, and the possession of such, for the entire human race. For example, the truth about material possessions is non-negotiable, they are only there to meet the basic needs of humanity and are not meant to be stored excessively; and no one should aspire to be popular other than as defenders of life, and only through Christ's methods. Each person must do all that they can to love one's neighbor, which does include a person's time and talent as well.

5

Countries, Particularly the United States, Must Lead
the Way to Creating a More Just (Christian) World

People who have an abundance of wealth and material possessions, are indeed most of the time, among the worst kind of players of the adult version of King of the Hill. They are not models of people following the teachings of Christ, especially in regards to the family and loving one's neighbor. Such people don't have a problem with having excess, when God-centered people go without the bear necessities in life, sometimes people from their own family. They fail to see their lack of compassion and the harm it causes. A lack of compassion leads to greed and because greed exists in our world the need for charity exists. The lack of love they have for neighbor is depressing.

People with excess oftentimes lack the creativity and vision to be charitable, or simply the motivation. Things like buying necessary clothes for your child or paying the rent for your apartment, so your family "can have a roof over their head," are not examples of excess. But when a couple, for example, has three cars, and a house with four bedrooms, for themselves and one very young child, they have to reconsider the reasons for having such. It could very quite possibly be that that couple is an obstacle to peace and justice. A smaller house would make more sense for this family; they could use the saved money to help others without any harm being done to their material needs.

People from the United States, for example, as a people, need to undergo a huge conversion with regard to excess; however, the problem with US conversion is two fold. First, it means giving up wealth and a world power status. Secondly, people from the US would need to accept being targets of retribution worldwide, for popular US culture has created resentment, and is a big reason why international conflict and war exists.

If people of the U.S. changed, if they became truly Christian, if they so desired, the most fundamental thing they would need to do would be indeed to shed and/or share their wealth sufficiently. When, for example, people from the US have savings in banking accounts that are larger than the amount of funds necessary to feed whole starving nations something is seriously wrong. To go in search of people worldwide, who are ready to do terrorist acts against Americans, in particular, while not addressing this type of injustice, reveals that the U.S. is not ready to take responsibility for their actions, and their contribution to the resentment that feeds terrorism.

There is one thing that goes hand and hand with Charity. It is usually reserved for what the Church calls the religious. It is monetary voluntary poverty. Charity and voluntary monetary poverty both stem directly from the Bible when new disciples were required to spread their wealth among all existing disciples, so everyone's needs are met.

Voluntary monetary poverty doesn't mean one's needs aren't met. It just means one is doing all he or she can so everyone else's needs are met. In fact Communist countries wouldn't have a reason to think in terms of being contrary to the US if only the US adopted Christ's virtue of charity completely enough.

Charity, also, doesn't have to be in just a handout fashion. People can be charitable creatively, even discriminately. Take pollution for example. It is a widespread problem in most countries. More rich people with great excess could do more to clean countries; they could use there excess to clean up these, poor and rich alike. They could hire unemployed and underemployed people to do the work. More people can be given the option to be empowered from having employment; they can be allowed the opportunity to help support themselves when before they had no work. A way to channel excess would be created and two large problems could be addressed. The rich could even keep there plans secret by working with governments so the people of nations didn't feel pitied, but employed.

The Catholic Church try's to communicate that if justice prevailed in the world charity wouldn't be necessary.

Those who seek to hoard money and resources (excess wealth), and to be popular in and for this world, are negligent and selfish, because of what they do or permit to happen in obtaining and/or maintaining their excess and/or status. The negligent and selfish(i.e. the greedy) are truly in great part responsible for the plight of the underemployed and unemployed, all of whom are fellow children of God.

People from the US must do what needs to be done to address the grievances of others at home and abroad through being just and charitable, which, after good personal morality, are the most loving actions a person can do in life, not out of fear but out of love, first and foremost from love of God which equates to love of neighbor (the Golden Rule). For without addressing greed from the US, which comes through indifference, frustration, fear, and hate, peace can never be achieved in the world. As a result, in the process of obtaining a false sense of security, greatness, and peace the people of the US give up being children of God.

It might be too much to ask of the US to change sufficiently without many people/and or countries seeking retribution for past policies based on greed, intimidation, and violence. However, without being ready to except the threat of physical harm, possibly even death, the Christian American can't know the peace of Christ.

6

Christian Leaders and the Roots of Christian Education

The lives of the people who resist the compulsion to be "of" this world everyday of their lives and to truly be Christian are truly remarkable. The greatest part of their lives consists of the work they do for their salvation and the salvation of others. They stay true to Christ through much persecution and even though everyone around them falters. They understand that attaining a place with Christ in the Father's Heavenly Kingdom is the most important aspect of existence, which is the direct result of a life in love for God and neighbor, which is everyone in the world.

The people who resist the compulsion to be "of" this world everyday of their lives understand the need to look at their faith life and the importance of good morals from a personal standpoint as well as from a communal one. If, for example, the person were the only believer left around her he or she needs do everything he or she could do to be a child of God even though no one around strives to be one, for the benefit of his or her personal relationship with God.

Most people who resist to be "of" this world seek the joy that comes from God and understand that injustice and corruption make impossible the attainment of joy. It's only by learning how to love, like through a resistance of excess things worldly, things transient, such as excess pleasure, many of life's comforts, false friendship, a false sense of security, anti-Christian popularity, and pure physical strength, taught by the love of Christ, that people attain joy.

These true Christians are fed by snippets of heavenly peace, the result of which is made possible from a life lived in the hope of being with God, and living to achieve that goal, which is made possible by living for God and neighbor. These true Christians capitalize upon the very goodness of others. They say thanks through prayer for real sacrifice. They focus on living moral and loving lives by asking the Lord to fill us with His Spirit, with His Grace, so we may one day be with Him in His Father's Heavenly Kingdom. True Christians do this because without being with Him they know they will never know joy. Christians, and Catholics in particular, must be repeatedly reminded that only with Him, through Him, and in Him we come to be.

It's sad when many of the most moral, loving, and faithful members of society, those of whom have little or no formal education, aren't modeled or listened to, because of their lack of formal education. It's especially sad that some, who are very moral and loving, for the good of others, aren't admired, appreciated, and/or respected.

People in the Church who are for the most part selfless don't have excess wealth, don't have worldly status other than as leaders for, of, and in Christ, aren't good friends with greatly immoral people, and do not have worldly power other than the power given to them by God, as leaders in, of, and for the Church. A world of moral and loving individuals, both personally and socially, is a world existing in true peace. It's a world that indeed looks very different from the one we live in; it's indeed a world that only our imaginations can grasp, not one ever experienced.

As mentioned beforehand, like with regard to responsible childbearing, a person doesn't have to have a lot of education, or the appropriate degree to follow good morals, to be loving, or to have correct strong Christian beliefs. In fact, on the contrary, a lot of education, more often than people are willing to admit, gets in the way of obtaining strong beliefs. Without faith, good morals, and love, a person can't be Christ-like and live, in particular, the Golden Rule. An education from schooling should only bring a person to have a deeper faith life to be more loving, and to have stronger good morals. People, for example, take the phrase "mind over matter" more seriously than it should be taken, when they should be thinking "the Holy Spirit is what gives matter meaning and purpose." The Holy Spirit will be the biggest advocate for your salvation.

In fact, it's the education a person receives at home which matters most to the development of good morals. It can also be said that, whether a person learns the importance of loving God and one's neighbor, the faith formation of an individual, primarily depends on one's home-life; in a best-case scenario education through schooling illuminates the deep appreciation for the Golden Rule, Christian morals one learns with one's family.

In the end all the education a person receives in life needs only to bring a person to accept the Truth, that Jesus Christ is the only Son of God, equal to God, and that Jesus came into the world to do what no pure human could do, save humanity from sin, that both God the Father and God the Son's love for humanity surpasses all human endeavors or ambitions, that humans need the Holy Spirit to be able to be His children; for without faith and faith in action, in making moral and loving decisions, a person is doomed.

For the more a person resists the temptation to worldliness the more joy that person experiences. If a person resists worldliness he or she can know love and love in return. It's by living for others, like through solid personal morals and like from the lack of hoarding, and especially by the abuse of others to achieve wealth and/or power, that people can become children of God, and not people who are without He who is the only true source of happiness and joy.

7

The Depths of the Immorality of Being Superficial

Truly not living the Golden Rule by hoarding excess wealth and seeking worldly status, which can come by the way of being superficial, contradicts the Catholic Church's teaching regarding the Golden Rule and loving one's neighbor. However, not many more times than none, living the Golden Rule, by working for justice and peace, are not considered moral issues. The mentalities, that abusing others to obtain excess wealth is okay, or from being popular through a disregard for God's laws, which are defining characteristics of the adult version of King of the Hill, are evil and very immoral, and happens way too often.

The people who hoard wealth and seek worldly status by being anti-Christian, who make obtaining justice and peace in the world very difficult, are as a result in great part responsible for the plight of the monetarily poor. They are so intoxicated by their excess, or from their ill achieved status, and from the support they receive from others playing this same game they never understand the need to embrace love for God and neighbor, and to live to empower all their brothers and sisters in Christ. Self-deception, as to what truly constitutes success, like living to be "kings" or "successful" people of this world, becomes almost instinctual.

Also in the process of hoarding money and resources, or from being popular from corrupt worldly status, people "block out the truth," oftentimes by offering excuses for their behavior. In the end, the confirmation people seek, from others living the same way(which definitely seems to be the majority of people in the world), is most of the time the only intoxicating support necessary to live the way they do. In doing so compassion is lost through what is really a false notion of "success," and salvation is dismissed as not being the most important aspect of a person's existence.

Sadly, by hoarding excess wealth and/or striving for what truly is anti-Christian worldly status, or by helping to provide others with those things, a person truly unites themselves with what is arguably the majority of people in the world. Those who love almost unconditionally are few and far between; Models of true Christian Love either are not appreciated or respected, or simply go unnoticed.

One excuse used in the process of hoarding money and resources, or from seeking worldly status, other than as children of God, is that a lot of people don't deserve just treatment. It's plausible that the need for charity wouldn't even exist if employers were completely responsible, for example, in giving just wages. However, sadly, the world economy is not based on justice stemming from Christian principles.

For example it doesn't make sense when, in the construction field, in the U.S. at least, a contractor feels the need to have the newest, biggest, most powerful, and most expensive truck on the market he or she can buy, when an older, smaller, less powerful, and less expensive truck is just as sufficient for his or her needs. By having the later and not the former a contractor could pay his or her laborer, or laborers, more, or what should be well, without worrying if he or she will not be able to ascertain life's necessities, and many unnecessary comforts. Sadly the truth is that all throughout the world laborer's rights are violated to a system of greed and to those who are power hungry.

Paying workers well doesn't mean everybody has to get the same, and certainly doesn't mean the US would be a Communistic state, language used by non-Christians to justify their greed, or as much as the contractor. It just means a person is being responsible and just in a Christ-like fashion.

Indeed, people don't have to revolutionize or worry about being, for example, a democrat or republican; all the have to do is improve and follow disciple to disciple guidelines outlined by Christ over 2000 years ago - the principles of meeting everyone's needs justly and charitably. It's equally important to understand that every person who can't accept sufficient as enough is guilty of believing that social morals don't exist.

The great conflict between worldliness and living for others can not be over emphasized. Living for others, the second part of the Golden Rule, means that a person resists the corruption (perversion) that comes from worldliness. People need to truly understand that living the Golden Rule can lead to a stronger relationship with God and personal joy, and is a requirement of those who would like to be with Christ in Heaven.

8

The Roots of the Anti-christian Divisions of Humanity

Players of the adult version of King of the Hill separate themselves from other players in the above-mentioned components. Some further sub-divisions are the different races, professions, education levels, and/or political affiliations.

People of these different sub-divisions oftentimes think that such affiliations entitle them to greater or lesser wealth and/or status, more so than people of other sub-divisions. Furthermore, if the sub-division includes the person knowing or having what is considered a skill or talent, that person oftentimes believes they are entitled to even more wealth and/or status.

The anti-Christian mentality, that worldly status and/or wealth matters, in and for itself, is a big reason why people suffer, and is why there is much conflict in the world. For skills and/or talents that are not in the service of the human race, even one's enemies, if one has any at all, go wasted. The biggest lie used by those seeking to obtain and/or maintain wealth and /or status is that God condones, and even supports, their actions, most prominently the ability to kill.

The problem with the King of the Hill world is that there are common cultural norms that run all throughout every country, regardless of divisions like in profession or political party. And even though different they might be on the surface, from one country to the next, much is similar in that that have anti-Christian characteristics.

Indeed, being anti-Christian, like by living for worldly wealth and/or status, one is contributing to conflict and war. The ultimate act of love is to shed all worldliness so that others can know peace and love, like what was asked of the rich man from the bible to do. Without justice and/or charity, you yourself doing them or supporting those who can, you can't say you're a follower of Christ.

All types of individuals play the adult version of King of the Hill. Those whom are deceived by those who deceive play it. It is played by the uneducated as well as the educated. But worst of all it is played by the conscientious as well as those who are not conscientious. The conscientious are the most hurtful and dangerous players of the adult King of the Hill game and, subsequently, are the biggest reason why there is injustice and chaos in the world. For anyone who knows between right and wrong, according to Christ and His Church, and chooses wrong, willfully, is truly dangerous; many people fall into this category.

For example, the conscientious are people who are fully aware of the evil in using others to achieve wealth and status to get ahead. They know it is wrong but still do it. In so doing they say no to God, neighbor, and anything that is good, for the sake of all that is death producing, a true reason for sorrow and pain.

Indeed, the adult version of King of the Hill is played by cultures, companies, governments, terrorists, armies, and/or countries, rich and poor alike. All such players have a mentality that is like the children who play King of the Hill, and which contributes to a chaotic world, that is founded on behavior that is madness. For people who act on their awareness of this worldly order, with love and compassion, wealth and worldly riches, in particular, are tools to meet their basic needs and the basic needs of the human race. Sharing one's wealth with one's neighbor, a person or persons of the human race, who doesn't have the bare necessities in life, and especially working for the glory of God, and not personal glory (status), are key ingredients to becoming a child of God. With this truth in mind the question is why should any person have excess? Why "sit" on money and resources, for example, that could save lives, the lives of many God-centered people, or seek to be backed by anti-Christian popular culture.

The message from Christ regarding treating others, even your enemies, like a brother or sister is not, for example, one of the mysteries of Catholicism, like the Trinity or transubstantiation. A lot of people like to think of the calling from Christ, to treat everyone like a brother or sister, as such. By doing so it's much easier to dismiss the Golden Rule as unimportant, because mysteries, which are supposed to be accepted on faith, to most people, are only congruent with physical entities and never touch. As a result truth and good morals, like the Golden Rule, are lost to an evil order of corruption and power and is the greatest reason why conflict, injustice, and chaos exists; the world order, indeed, is able to function the way it does because people in the world are able to dismiss the teachings of Christ and His disciples. In other words, it's by dismissing aspects of Christianity, especially the Golden Rule people worldwide can work, support, and/or fight to maintain the chaotic world, in which we live, the defining feature of the King of the Hill world.

9

Bad Decision Making Regarding Childbearing

A huge obstacle preventing the communion of all of God's children comes from a misunderstanding, particularly by the monetarily poor, of the phrases from the bible "happy are the poor in spirit" and "be fertile and multiply," as if just by being monetarily poor with many children assures a person a place in heaven, that God reigns more strongly with people whom go without the bare necessities in life, just because they struggle for the bare necessities; it's seems as if they think happiness comes with struggling to put food "on the table," "clothes on the back," and an adequate place to live for your children. In fact, along with the rich hoarding enormous amounts of excess, and using others to achieve it, injustice and war, defining characteristics of the King of the Hill world, can be attributed to bad decision-making in childbearing. There are so many people so destitute monetarily that becoming empowered to love one's neighbor, as being one's top priority, is very difficult to understand and embrace as a way of life.

Firstly, it's very important not to confuse the result of irresponsible childbearing, monetary poverty, with the happiness that Jesus talks about from being poor in spirit. The word spirit has two totally different meanings when talking about poor in spirit and the Holy Spirit. Poor in spirit implies little interest in worldly things, like wealth and/or status not poor in the Holy Spirit

Secondly, in the Bible, in the Old Testament, God tells Adam and Eve (or the descendants of Abraham will be like that of the stars of the sky) to "be fertile and multiply." This mandate from God to Adam and Eve is thought as true even today. People fail to understand that when God willed Adam and Eve to be fertile and multiply there were only two people on earth. Two people, with, literally, all the land in the world and all it's resources. They did not have to consider overpopulation in a world where the economy is based on profiteering. The world did not consist of people with billions in excess and many people starving. A person committed to peace will make responsible choices about childbearing, based on sacrifice/ love.

Too often, when a person has many children, that person is not bothered by the fact that one or two of their children is struggling to earn enough to obtain the bare necessities. If a person is not willing and/or capable to support a child his or her whole life, if need be, that person shouldn't have a child, a sad reality among the world's billions. The problem is even worse when a person is unwilling and incapable to support a child, his or her whole life, if need be, and has multiple children. Whereas in Adam and Eve's day it wasn't necessary today one needs to consider the ability to support a child, where support continues for the duration of a parent's life, if need be; it's due to the difficulty in finding valuable and reliable life sustaining work a person seriously needs to think hard before bringing a child into this world. For although being poor monetarily allows people greater opportunity to learn the value of being poor in spirit, to which Jesus allude's in the Surman on the Mount, than there is from being rich, it doesn't mean that if you are poor, monetarily or otherwise, you are automatically are going to have a strong relationship with God.

You will not hear the truth about "be fertile and multiply" in school, in most churches, or even from most day to day ordinary people. However a person doesn't need to wait until a teacher, a priest, a biblical scholar, or expert on morality tells you that the mandate from God, to be fertile and multiply, for most people, does not exist in the twenty first century.

The problem with having more children than a person can support indeed has to do with the fact that there are many more people looking for work then there are good jobs that pay well available. This should be basic economic knowledge anybody who intends to have children should except and respect before they decide that they can have children. This is the reason why a person can not bring a child into this world unless they are ready and willing to support that child for the duration of the child's life, until death, if need be, because of the difficulty in finding reliable life sustaining work.

Indeed there are many more people in the world that, even though quite capable, can't find work, or at least adequate work. Employees, as a result, have the option to get away with paying unjust wages because of the number of capable people willing to work for less. Players of the adult version of King of the Hill aren't bothered that there are many more people who need good jobs that pay well then there are good jobs that pay well available.

When people have more children then they can support children suffer. For children need housing that meets their needs relative to their needs within the context of the nuclear family, with two parents ready, financially, psychologically, and spiritually to raise them to be strong children in, of, and for God.

Children need space to grow and move without problems within the family, which relates to the need for security. Adequate housing also helps protect children against things like adverse climate. Children need to have nutritious meals of a sufficient quantity each day. Children need clothing and a means for cleanliness, because cleanliness helps protect against sickness and disease. But most importantly children need loving family members who strive to grow in doing the right thing based on the communion of all of God's children.

All together, with justice and charity, solid personal morals, including responsible childbearing, the world could look very different from the one we live in and would be much different than any that ever existed; and at the same time, by having solid personal morals, by being just and charitable, and by being responsible in childbearing a person is doing all he or she can in doing his or her part in the salvation plan. Solid personal morals, justice and charity, and responsible child-bearing are indeed the keys also to becoming a child of God and are needed to achieve peace on earth.

The person who is responsible in childbearing is content even though in many cases the person has to endure hardship; he or she is content despite hardship. He or she is fed on the very notion of peace without ever knowing it, completely.

The Catholic Church has concrete solutions to the problem with childbearing when taking into consideration over-population in the world. The first, and the more difficult choice, is abstinence. The second, which also requires discipline, is natural family planning. Natural family planning involves timing in the month, between a married couple, based on a women's menstrual cycle, it is least likely that the women will become pregnant from intercourse.

It doesn't matter if a person is among the rich who hoard or monetarily poor people who act irresponsibly in childbearing, people who choose to be hurtful, possibly because they have been hurt, need to stop the cycle of pain, by accepting the grace of God and act on it appropriately.

10

Poverty of the Holy Spirit, Grace, and God's Gifts

The path in the life of Christ, to live counter culturally lovingly and peacefully, to lead communities out of the destitution of the King of the Hill mentality, is the most difficult path in life a person can take. Oftentimes people stumble because they don't recognize the love of Christ that is transmitted to them by the Holy Spirit, through the Grace of God. With the Holy Spirit a person can recognize their full potential to live in harmony with the human race, and, as a result, in becoming a child of God. People don't understand that by being children of God they have reached the climax of existence, which is an existence they must keep striving to rediscover their whole life.

Truth is told, the problem with many people who play the adult version of King of the Hill, maybe even most people who play, is that they have a severe poverty of the Holy Spirit. Such people try to substitute the peace, acquired by being filled with the Holy Spirit, with feeling good from having excess wealth and/or status.

In fact people don't take seriously the importance of being counter cultural, lovingly and peacefully. For example, if you can't see, or don't want to accept, the truth behind popular culture, like materialism and greed in and from the US, or irresponsible child-bearing like among the poor, you don't understand Christ's message regarding following Him.

People with a poverty of the Holy Spirit are much less likely to make moral loving decisions, and immoral unloving decisions lead to a poverty of the Holy Spirit. At this point in a person's life, when a person is in a state of a poverty of the Holy Spirit something from outside the person needs to intervene to stop this viscous cycle of the poverty of the Holy Spirit, within the worldly person, because these people, in this viscous cycle, can not change on their own; people with a poverty of the Holy Spirit indeed need God's Grace.

Most people are afraid of the change necessary to bring about justice and peace, afraid oftentimes that if they let their guard down they might get hurt. Or if someone recognizes the need for change, in whatever venue of life, in themselves, their family, their country, and the world, after determining change is needed, most of the time they feel powerless to bring it about, and they give up trying to be a moral loving individual. Also it seems as if people do not know what to do in a world of justice and peace, like maybe they're not worthy of it at a particular time.

Indeed to bring about justice and peace people must learn to forgo anything material in exces, monetarily or otherwise, excess comfort, popularity from an immoral worldly status, a false sense of security, and unhealthy pleasure. People need to understand, or should except, that the obstacles to change, however great they may be, are worth the effort and can equate to the reality of inner peace and/or a better world. Furthermore, if people understood the relationship between justice and peace and the importance of those entities for the salvation of their souls then change would be much more likely to occur. Again, the intervention of Grace is needed if a person can't make changes on his or her own.

It's exactly when temptation arrives, after people learn that their actions are connected to their salvation, the need for change is most important. And it doesn't matter if Grace comes in the form of a person or motivating force from another person or persons, both are gifts from God.

Grace indeed comes to people in the form of gifts. The person, who uses God's gift, or gifts, knows not, for example, to condescend another's – God's gift of Grace is what makes a person harmonious with the human race. The person who recognizes God's gift as a sign of God's love for His children, to fill His children with love, is motivated to act in accord with God's will. It is only by using God's Grace one can consider himself or herself loving in a Christian fashion and can be described as a person who acts in accord with God's will and uses, for example, free-will correctly.

Joy, which is a by-product of love, can be, for example, the result of the Holy Spirit lived, in Christ, by good morals, which is love for one's neighbor. The gift of grace provides people with the opportunity to have a valuable identity. At best joy will become addictive to the individual committed to God and Communion through His Grace.

Grace is needed to help a person become a child of God and not of the world. First, a person needs to have an offer of Grace to them by God. Each and every person has to be ready to accept and use the gift of God's Grace (we must pray so that we are ready to use an offer of Grace to us.), because to follow His will is to say yes to His will. Then the person needs to accept the offer by using God's Grace.

The person who accepts an offer of Grace from God, and uses It, is by so doing choosing to be more filled with the Holy Spirit. From there a person can start to "climb out of the hole" of that which was created from their actions in conjunction with their previous poverty of the Holy Spirit. This is how the vicious cycle of a poverty of the Holy Spirit, connected with immoral unloving actions, can start to be eliminated.

The Holy Spirit is from God Himself. The Holy Spirit was ushered into the world through the door that is Jesus Christ, our Lord and Savior, as humanity's Gift, by His sacrifice, realized through faith.

Oftentimes people inherit a poverty of the Holy Spirit, at least indirectly, because others have hurt them in their lives, sometimes by a person or persons close to them. People who have been hurt oftentimes internalize their pain and bottle it up within themselves(for example, by seeking immoral worldly wealth and/or power). Or they intoxicate themselves so they don't have to deal with their pain. Sometimes people who have been hurt in their lives reproduce the pain through actions that cause pain, with more vigor than those who are the reason for their pain did to them. Oftentimes people do this because they believe they have no other option available. This is a big reason why we live in a world that sometimes lacks compassion and love. This cycle of a lack of Love, the foundation of the adult version King of the Hill world, is why we live in a world that sees sometimes conflict and war.

Only a Christ-like approach to the problems in the world, through the Holy Spirit, can lead to our salvation, of the little part of which we partake, and which subsequently will lead to inner peace and peace in the world. The Holy Spirit helps people to live good morals and to love, for example, by directing a person in the appropriate use of free will; with the Holy Spirit one knows love and is content.

11

Freedom, Free-will, and the Universal Community

People, as alluded to previously, sometimes are not loving and live bad morals because they are confused about freedom and free-will; anything that is an option in life is seen as an acceptable choice, that because they have the option to deviate from God's will, particularly when many people do, that is acceptable to God to make that choice. People fail to understand that the only reason free-will exists is so a person may know love.

People need to understand that God allows people to to deviate from His will, and forbids them to do so, at the same time. Even bad morals, for example, which are contrary to love, are not thought of as bad, just because they are an option. As a result pleasure is chosen over joy, greed over justice, and violence over peace and Love. However, it's only by following God's will, through accepting God's invitation to Love, one can say yes to God's invitation to salvation, and to be strong for the world.

Many times people ill-use free will or dismiss the importance of being Christian because they overemphasize the importance of being unique.

Being unique is important. However, too many people in the world worry about being unique first when God is calling each one of us to be like His Son first and then unique.

For even though it's true that everyone is unique a person's uniqueness is not more important than their shared identity in the community of believers who are united in their Christian characteristics; and truly, if someone wishes to be unique, it should be because they model Christ well, because they are filled with the Holy Spirit and in reality love in the manner Christ wants us to, which most people would probably characterize as being unique.

One can be unique in their worldliness or unique in their love for others. In fact it doesn't make sense to most people, or they don't quite understand the importance, that in order to obtain value as an individual one must be like so many who have walked the earth before, saints and others. Moreover, to ascertain peace of mind and peace of heart one must be exactly like countless others who live, and have lived, and the common characteristic they share, or shared, that made them whole – that of the immense love they had for God and neighbor.

People shy away from working for an identification exactly the same of other strong models of Christ, those dedicated to community through celebration of the Sacraments, because they don't understand the importance of the Universal communion of all believers in Christ. In exchange people seek "kingship" of their homes, families, work, or any venue where "kingship" is attainable.

People need to surrender to God's will and embrace the One, True, Faith.

The truth is it is certainly much easier to justify worldliness if one's philosophy doesn't include loving others, including one's enemies. However, sadly, there just aren't enough people of a Christian conscience to change the non-Christian popular cultures in the world; change indeed is difficult because there are so many people that don't have a problem saying that they are not religious, Christian, they are atheistic, or they have incorrect morals. In fact hell on earth, which is possible, is the sum total of the decay of the moral integrity of humanity, from weak relationships with God. The only solution is to embrace and cling to God and never let go. Let Him be the food that nourishes you and which provides you with Life.

For starters all world powers, for example the United States, need to lead the way in the world by adopting a complete Christian way of life. The only way to change the "American Way," for example, and end the King of the Hill mentality a person has to be a God-centered individual with good morals, which includes working for just wages, and, by being charitable. Again, this means you put others before yourself and do what you can to even create peace and justice even for your enemies, if one has any(With regard to one's enemies, the goal should be to facilitate a transformation of enemies to becoming your brothers and/or sisters in Christ). The more detached the people who make up governments are, for example, from the true message of Christ the more problematic that society, and the world, will be.

In a world where people made following good morals a priority strength, for example, would be by one's actions in line with peace, justice, compassion and love, not worldly success like wealth and/or corrupt status, or by supplying others with worldly wealth and/or corrupt status; a strong person is so because of he or she embodies peace, justice, and love for everyone.

It hurts God that people don't testify to His Love through building a stronger community, for the greatest union is the shared identity of the believers in Christ. If the working man, for example, was Christ-like in his approach to his business everyone's needs would be met in this world and there would not be any conflict and war (responsible child-bearing would need to occur also). For true Christians there's no need for competition or domination, only an existence in the world where every body lived in harmony with the other person and all people.

Voluntary monetary poverty, as well, as mentioned beforehand, which truly is a calling to all of Christ's followers, is instrumental and necessary to a world in peace. Voluntary monetary poverty exists so everyone in the world has all that they need in life to flourish. However, as also pointed out beforehand, the problem with our world economy is that it is founded on profiteering and not on love. Even though the calling to voluntary monetary poverty comes from Christ Himself, and is one of the most important Christian mandates, it is not followed. Most people simply dismiss voluntary monetary poverty as an unrealistic idealistic way of life reserved only for the "religious," but in reality it is the true key to peace in a world where sacrifice is the exemption and not the rule, and interpreted to mean the giving of one's life in battle, like battles are inevitable and can't be avoided by other sacrifices.

A world of moral individuals, both personally and socially, is a world existing in peace, love, and true peace. It's a world that looks very different from the one we live in; it's a world that only our imaginations can grasp, not one ever experienced. However, if we strive to be Christ-like through following good morals and by loving God and neighbor we, at least, can know peace.

The experience of peace and joy is God's way of reinforcing loving/moral behavior. The evidence that a person is experiencing peace and joy can be seen in a person's demeanor. A person following both personal and social morals is tranquil, and often-times, pleasant. The joy is there and the person sabers it and holds on to it as long as possible by not thinking or doing anything else. And after the saber of joy from that experience dies out a person strong in the Holy Spirit continues living the Golden Rule in pursuit of the next experience of joy, until death.

12

Highlight of Major Themes

To look a person, or group of people, in the world in terms of us and them is a total contradiction to the worldview posited by Christ Himself. Moreover, it's sad when people accept as sufficient the greatness that this world can provide them. These "this world only" individuals do not have God in their lives and are at a lost without Him. It's people who are not Christian, who are hurtful, who concentrate on the present world only, or even just first, before the eternal, who consider friends in relation to unhealthy worldliness, to achieve wealth and/or corrupt status in and for themselves, particularly to help one's nation be at "the top" by anti-Christian methods, if only to just be "on top" of one other country (or two or more others) and to not live a life in love for God and neighbor, and who don't stick to the rules of God outlined by the Church's family based philosophy, for the entire human race, who are agents of upheaval.

Though one person or country, or even all of humanity, may resist the will of God a total surrendering of each entity's will to

His will bring the entity back to a peaceful existence. Most importantly, it is the will of God to adhere to the Golden Rule, which conscripts us to a life in God through a life for others, eventually to all of humanity, the total giving of one's time, talent, and treasure for all of God's children, even people who we think don't deserve our time, talent, and treasure, to help everyone and all nations be strong.

For example, selfless people are not paranoid and defensive about their skills or talents, if their skills or talents come from Him. They know that any skill or talent not directed toward the benefit of others, even one's enemies, is a wasted skill or talent. People devoid of the love of God with great talent are very harmful toward a society meant for that love. Such people do not seek the glorification of God but rather their own status as "winners" or "successful" people. Any person who does not acknowledge their skill or talent as a gift from God, if that skill or talent is indeed from Him, and in turn use it or them for the betterment of humanity, is wasting that which was given for humanity.

It can not be stressed enough, more importantly than meeting a person's basic needs, the purpose of material goods and bodily functions, and talents employed to achieve such, is to help a person arrive at a state of existence that best host the Spirit of God. The use of such otherwise is an ill use of those things meant to help a person arrive at that which we were designed to be, that as children of God. The most effective way to create peace is indeed through being moral and loving and by dedicating your life to the entire human race, not by being blind to sin from being unduly patriotic, especially when one's motive's are to do harm to another, or if a country has great fault(s).

The mark of a good effort to establish a peaceful co-existence of all mankind is tranquility in those who work for it. This person knows that there's no room for secularism and unhealthy nationalism. It can be dangerous when a person primarily defines him or her self by their worldly titles, and not as Christian. He or she knows to be a family oriented person and to be responsible in childbearing, if childbearing is in God's plan for you. For he or she knows Christ does not recognize the value in cultural norms just for the sake of being among the majority; He doesn't share views with others about the aspects of culture, other than aspects which are from Him, that make it good, and He especially doesn't consider one's history when distributing His love and mercy.

Two words to sum up our Christian mission here on earth are brotherhood and sisterhood. Christian brotherhood and sisterhood mean to live for all mankind. The person who works for brotherhood and sisterhood sees the joy that can be gained even though working for brotherhood and sisterhood might mean becoming a target of retribution. The glorification of God is sought after as the means by which one obtains joy on earth and eternal salvation.

The most important tenet of Christianity has to do with the mistakes we make in trying to bring peace to ourselves and those around us, to an imperfect world, when we don't let God intercede through us. That because our efforts will ultimately always bring us short of Heaven, we need the salvation won for us by God's only begotten Son. And even though it's impossible to obtain perfect peace and joy here on earth people can not give up on God, or working for Him, and the Universal Communion that the Church defends. In the process of trying to defend the Universal Communion of the believers of say the Trinity people can't give up working for the Sacraments, they are the median by which we obtain our salvation. We must always remember that we can not save our selves, or others, but we can definitely cause harm to the chances of such.

One can not be deterred from a life in the Church by the imperfections of those who make it up. Even though there are big problems in the Church because of the imperfections of some of its members there is at least equal amount goodness in the Church because of the goodness of others who are for the most part good. Form an allegiance with those members of the Church who won't let you down. Seek their friendship and permit them to be your leaders.

It's a lot to ask for of human weakness but people definitely have to forgo things, like mentioned beforehand, unhealthy excitement, excess pleasure, worldly wealth, excess comfort, false security, and false pride. Asking humanity to forgo those things is like trying to ask a person to swim against a strong tide or to stay out in the cold when it's freezing. Everything that's natural directs us to be contrary to God. And it's frustrating oftentimes to make a difference in the world, which a moral and loving individual might want to do, when he or she feels he or she doesn't have much to work with, possibly no wealth, status, education, or influence which comes from a healthy popularity with others. However, the truth is that everyone does matter to God, so "getting ahead" can't be to the detriment of anyone, physically, mentally, or spiritually.

Those people in our world who are filled with the Holy Spirit to live for all of humanity understand that our purpose here on earth is greater than any one person's personal plan or goals; we live for one purposeful entity made possible by a collective effort, even though the value of our Church comes only by the strength of our members.

Although people waver in good morals, no matter how gravely, there is always the possibility of reconciliation back to the flock, back to a unity of the masses the value of to which the amount of peace in the world can only testify. The crux, though, is that reconciliation is the work we must partake in order to obtain peace and justice; peace and justice takes work, a complete surrendering to God's Will.

Instead of working side by side to maintain the madness of the King of the Hill world people must work toward side by side in creating a world like none that ever existed, which is done by following the complete message from Christ, to create world peace not world dominance. People must be unique in so much that they are they filled with the Holy Spirit and a love for all of the world's brothers and sisters, through solid personal and social morals and by, for those with the calling, to be responsible in childbearing. Creating a world like none that ever existed is entirely tied into your eternal salvation, and one's eternal salvation, whether people know and/or accept it, is the most important thing worth living for. The truth can not be under-understood, in addition to solid personal morals one's eternal salvation hinges upon one's profound commitment to justice and peace, and by being, again, for those with the calling, responsible in childbearing.

Players of the adult version of King of the Hill don't really understand that the greatest source of joy, here on earth and in Heaven, is God. Happiness, which gets confused with joy, by the pursuit of things like wealth and/or corrupt status, is completely different and less than joy. For the problem, in addition to what people are willing to do to get "on the top," has to do with what people are willing to do to stay there. We aren't perfect, we do have imperfections that cause conflict and war in the world, so we need the salvation won for us by Christ, a salvation which is made possible through Communion and the Church.

After reconciling one's past, by "coming to terms" with one's past, choices must be made to commit or recommit to following God's will. People indeed need, for example, to look at their faith life and the importance of good morals from a personal standpoint as well as from a communal one. People indeed need the help of God's Grace. If, for example, as noted before, the person were the only believer left on the earth he or she needs do everything he or she could do to be a child of God even though no one else strives to be one, for the benefit of his or her personal relationship with God and his or her salvation.

The most important reason to live good morals is, paradoxically, to do the small part that a person can do in the salvation plan (this belief is where the Catholic Church differs from other Christian denominations). The other two reasons, addressed before hand, to have good morals, is to make possible a life of peace for one self while here on earth and to make more peace and justice possible for others in a world lacking compassion, justice, and peace.

One day we will face our Creator and He will ask us if we dedicated our lives to all our brothers and sisters in the world, focusing particularly on the poor and one's "enemies." He will wonder if we were players of the adult version of King of the Hill and as a result were guilty of using others for worldliness. He will wonder if we saw the evil behind worldliness and it's importance to our eternal existence, even for some the importance of our very lives here on earth.

People need to see that it's good morals that will make your country strong not false pride that impedes a person's ability to "see" that which is truly valuable in life, which is a strong relationship with our Creator and all of humanity.

The virtue of charity, as difficult as it is to except, demands of us to be charitable, unto the giving for some our very lives. Don't be afraid of change to bring about a more just society, especially don't send another person to kill, or be killed, in your name. To create, work for, support and/or fight for a particular system, not founded on God, and not through His methods, just to prove that another system is unjust, for example, won't work.

In the end everyone will die, the only question is how and for what purpose. Even the poorest peasant of any developing nation can be a value to their country by converting to and embracing a Christian ideology that gives richness to life and enhances life regardless of political ideology. Christ is the savior of everyone in the world, citizens of Democracies and Communistic nations, capitalists and socialist, poor and rich people, people with worldly power and people with none. The goal should be to be a part of a movement connected to real peace through real mercy and charity. Some people argue some governments are better suited to bring about the kingdom of God, but in reality only people of the "nation" of God can bring about the kingdom of God.

End

King of the Hill – Why? Why play it? Why? Why do what a vast majority of people have done, and continue to do, since the beginning of time? Why not do the hard thing in life? Is not your soul and eternal existence of more importance than anything else?

Christ's full mandate in loving one's neighbor isn't embraced by the pursuit of excess wealth and/or the pursuit of a status as anything else but being one of His children. Injustice, with regard to just wages, through not being charitable, and irresponsible childbearing, within and without marriage, are the gravest problems harming justice and peace and are the biggest reasons why conflict and war exist. North Americans, for example, can't get involved in a quest to establish security against a people seeking to become more powerful in the world. Paradoxically, a person or people whom seek to do harm, must be allowed to do harm if being harmed is unavoidable. Prepare to defend yourself first and foremost by prayer and by working to have a strong relationship with God. Then concentrate on being strong in other aspects of your life.

There are no exceptions God loves everyone. A person who "knows" that God loves everyone strives to love everyone in return, even one's "enemies." A person will "know" love when he or she feels like giving his or her life for his or her "enemy," not taking his or hers.

If the parameters of the King of the Hill game were completely different everyone should play.

The goal of a King of the Hill game everyone should play would be to try and bring everyone you can to Heaven with you. The rules of this game that everyone should play would be the same as they've always been, as set down by Christ.

In a King of the Hill game that everyone should play Christ would be at the top of the Hill, like He was on Calvary and is now with the Father in Heaven. The object of the game would be to share both "Hills" with Christ, first each person's Calvary then Heaven. Only after reaching their Calvary can a person reach Heaven and be with Him and the Father. To reach Calvary one must be the servant of others, for starters, by following the Golden Rule, the greatest commandment; the holiest people in the world are people not afraid to sacrifice day in and day out. In this version of King of the Hill the greatest servant gets to share the "Hill" with Christ and the Father the soonest, with all others sharing the "Hill" already, like our blessed mother.

The word Communion alone sums up the Catholic Church's mission here on earth, which is to bring about a harmonious existence among all people all over the world, "enemies" as much as friends through becoming more like Christ. No other religion, or denomination of Christianity, proposes this kind of philosophy, or mission, as it's means of existence and goal, quite like the Catholic Church.

No one should attempt to reinvent the rules; for example neither politics nor personal temptations should get in the way of working towards the glory of God. To be honest about where ones efforts should be spent takes oftentimes a lot of humility. To be among the masses of people with no profound daily impact on world events is not something to dwell on and about which to despair - Everyone does indeed matter to Jesus and can impact the lives of those around them, even if one's sole contribution is recognizing one's need for mercy and Grace.

The fastest way to become the greatest servant is to imitate Christ and others who are Christ-like by denying worldly wealth and repute, even most of the time of even being considered by others as being holy, so that everyone can share the "Hill" with Christ. Getting to Heaven through Calvary means breaking down all the dynamics of the King of the Hill game that need to be accepted for what adverse purpose they serve, which eventually means that a person must reject the adult version of King of the Hill and all it stands. Being the greatest servant means picking up one's cross everyday of life without letting people know the difficulty in doing so, without begrudging every step, and celebrating and worshiping with others, which is to strengthen one's personal relationship with God. It's by living out the Golden Rule through Communion, through receiving Him through the Grace of the Holy Spirit, namely through the Eucharist.

It is necessary for each person in every society, of every socioeconomic status, even regardless of differences in things like religion and world philosophy, of those seeking worldly wealth and people who try to seek reputations in this world other than as His children, to convert to and embrace the kind of Love Christ embodied, which is characterized by good morals and sacrifice, a philosophy coincidentally which can only come through faith in Jesus Christ and His Church; the true life of a Christian is indeed a life of good morals and charity, which is to peacefully protest the King of the Hill mentality.

Everyone is loved; everyone is called to follow Him, His actions, and His message. Everyone is invited to His joy through a conscientious decision to say yes to His and His Father's will through the help of Grace, particularly the Holy Spirit.

The trick in living a faithful life and doing the right thing is to be persistent because most times faith and good morals are not rewarded. It's too easy to loose heart and come to the conclusion that doing the right thing just isn't worth the effort. However, everyone should strive to be a part of something more meaningful, something more detached from the apathy, frustration, and hate exists in this world. For Love conquers all, and leaves all apathy, frustration, and hate behind leaving only the cherished existence of a brother and sisterhood only the heavenly understand.

Those who are moral and loving through persistence experience the joy that can only come from heaven. That's why it's important to be persistent, not to loose faith, and for Catholics, to receive the Eucharist at all times possible. Every occasion of joy from being moral and loving only solidifies the person's persistence and commitment and consistency in Love.

The bottom line is that Jesus came into His Fathers world to save, to offer humanity the option of salvation. We do need to try and make the world better, but in the end, Jesus, as the instrument of salvation, is the only One, through the Holy Spirit, who can make the world a world of peace and justice; the yes to God's invitation is ironically that we need to pray that He eradicate the King of the Hill mentality and bring love and peace to mankind.

For the people who live for this world will be "Kings" in this world and will long to serve in the next.